Benjamin Franklin

By Philip Abraham

Welcome
Books

Children's Press®
A Division of Scholastic Inc.
New York / Toronto / London / Auckland / Sydney
Mexico City / New Delhi / Hong Kong
Danbury, Connecticut

Photo Credits: Cover © The Corcoran Gallery of Art/Corbis; p. 5 © Francis G. Mayer/Corbis; p. 7 © Corbis; pp. 9, 11, 15, 17, 19, 21 © Bettmann/Corbis; p. 13 © Hulton/Archive by Getty Images

Contributing Editor: Jennifer Silate
Book Design: Christopher Logan

Library of Congress Cataloging-in-Publication Data

Abraham, Philip, 1970–
Benjamin Franklin / by Philip Abraham.
    p. cm. -- (Real people)
Includes index.
Summary: An easy-to-read biography of the man who was a publisher, inventor, scientist, and one of
    the authors of the Declaration of Independence.
  ISBN 0-516-23954-6 (lib. bdg.) -- ISBN 0-516-23601-6 (pbk.)
   1. Franklin, Benjamin, 1706–1790--Juvenile literature. 2. Statesmen--United States--Biography--
    Juvenile literature. 3. Scientists--United States--Biography--Juvenile literature. 4. Inventors--United
    States--Biography--Juvenile literature. 5. Printers--United States--Biography--Juvenile literature.
    [1. Franklin, Benjamin, 1706–1790. 2. Statesmen. 3. Scientists. 4. Inventors. 5. Printers.] I. Title. II.
    Real people (Children's Press)

E302.6.F8 A185 2002
973.3'092--dc21
[B]   2001047086

Contents

Meet Benjamin Franklin.

Benjamin was born on January 17, 1706.

5

Benjamin grew up in Boston, Massachusetts.

As a boy, Benjamin worked for his older brother, James.

James owned a printing shop.

9

Benjamin became a very good **printer**.

Soon, he opened his own printing shop.

He printed books and newspapers.

Poor Richard, 1740.

Polly AN *Caffard's*

Almanack

For the Year of Chrift

1740,

Being **LEAP YEAR.**

And makes fince the Creation	Years.
By the Account of the Eaftern *Greeks*	7248
By the Latin Church, when ☉ ent. ♈	6939
By the Computation of *W. W.*	5749
By the *Roman* Chronology	5689
By the *Jewifh* Rabbies	5501

Wherein is contained,

The Lunations, Eclipfes, Judgment of the Weather, Spring Tides, Planets Motions & mutual Afpects, Sun and Moon's Rifing and Setting, Length of Days, Time of High Water, Fairs, Courts, and obfervable Days.

Fitted to the Latitude of Forty Degrees, and a Meridian of Five Hours Weft from *London*, but may without fenfible Error, ferve all the adjacent Places, even from *Newfoundland* to *South-Carolina*.

By *RICHARD SAUNDERS*, Philom.

PHILADELPHIA:
Printed and fold by *B. FRANKLIN*, at the New Printing-Office near the Market.

Benjamin loved to read.

He helped start the first **library** in the United States.

Benjamin was also good at **science**.

He liked to study **electricity**.

15

Benjamin was a very good writer, too.

He helped write the **Declaration of Independence**.

19

Benjamin Franklin did many important things.

We will always remember him.

21

New Words

Declaration of Independence (dek-luh-**ray**-shuhn **uhv** in-di-**pen**-duhnss) the public statement made on July 4, 1776, in which the American colonies declared themselves free from Great Britain

electricity (i-lek-**triss**-uh-tee) energy that produces heat, light, or motion

inventor (in-**ven**-tuhr) a person who makes or thinks of new things

library (**lye**-brer-ee) a place where books are kept for people to use and borrow

printer (**prin**-tuhr) a person who makes books, magazines, or newspapers

science (**sye**-uhnss) a system of gathering knowledge, using observations and experiments

To Find Out More

Books
A Picture Book of Benjamin Franklin
by David A. Adler
Holiday House

Benjamin Franklin: A Photo-Illustrated Biography
by T. M. Usel
Bridgestone Books

Web Site
The Electric Ben Franklin
http://ushistory.org/franklin/
This site includes a biography of Benjamin Franklin, quotations,
a timeline, and fun puzzles and games.

Index

About the Author
Philip Abraham is a freelance writer. He works in New York City.

Reading Consultants
Kris Flynn, Coordinator, Small School District Literacy, The San Diego County Office of Education

Shelly Forys, Certified Reading Recovery Specialist, W.J. Zahnow Elementary School, Waterloo, IL

Sue McAdams, Former President of the North Texas Reading Council of the IRA, and Early Literary Consultant, Dallas, TX